Ri

Written by Susan James

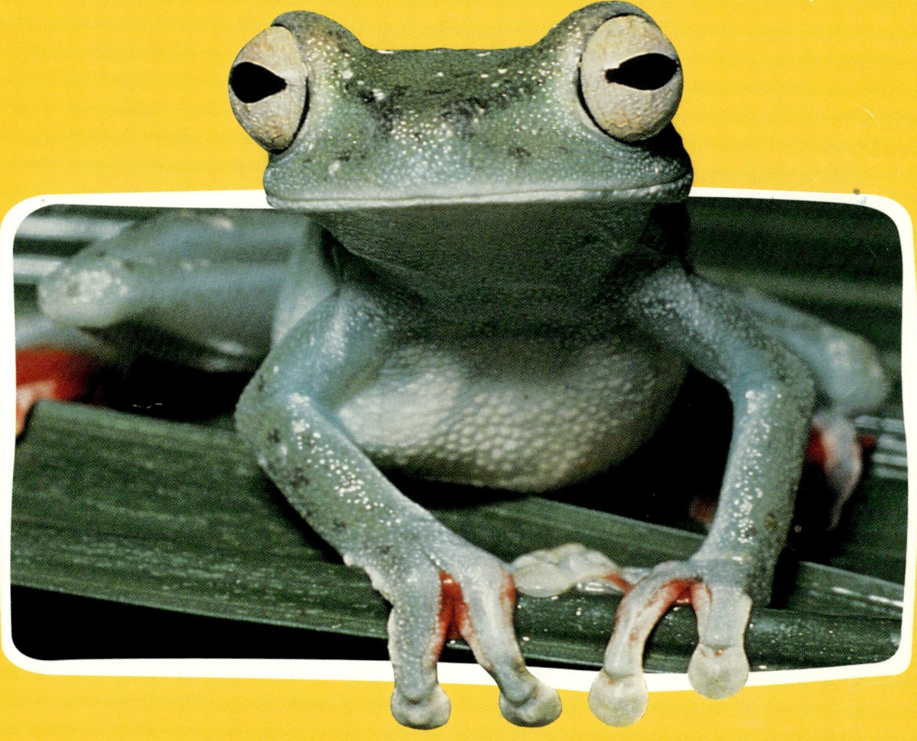

Celebration Press

An Imprint of Addison -Wesley
Educational Publishers, Inc.

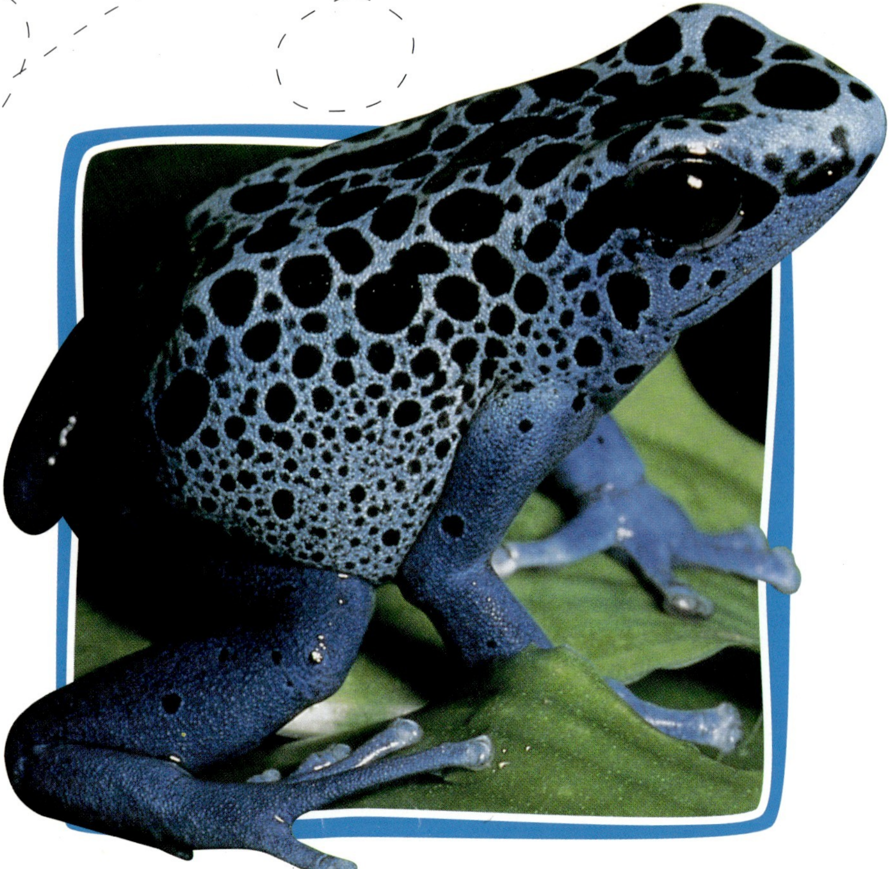

Ribbit!

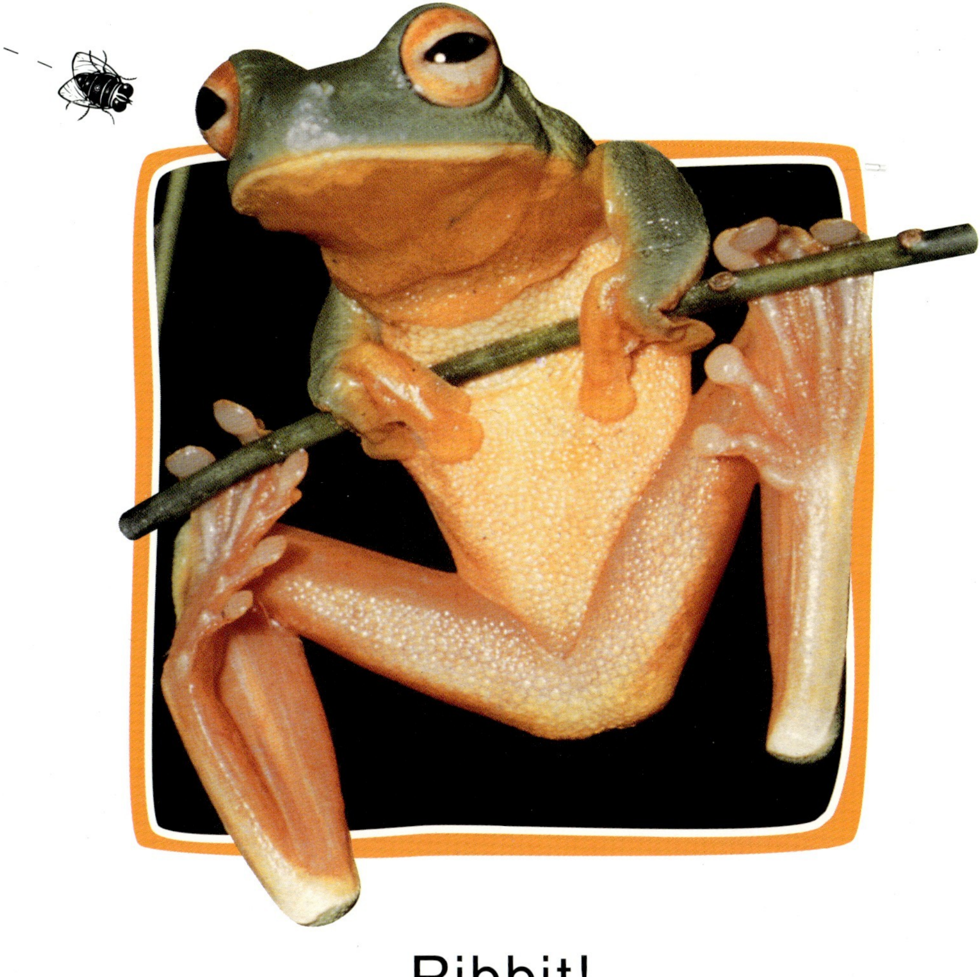

Ribbit!

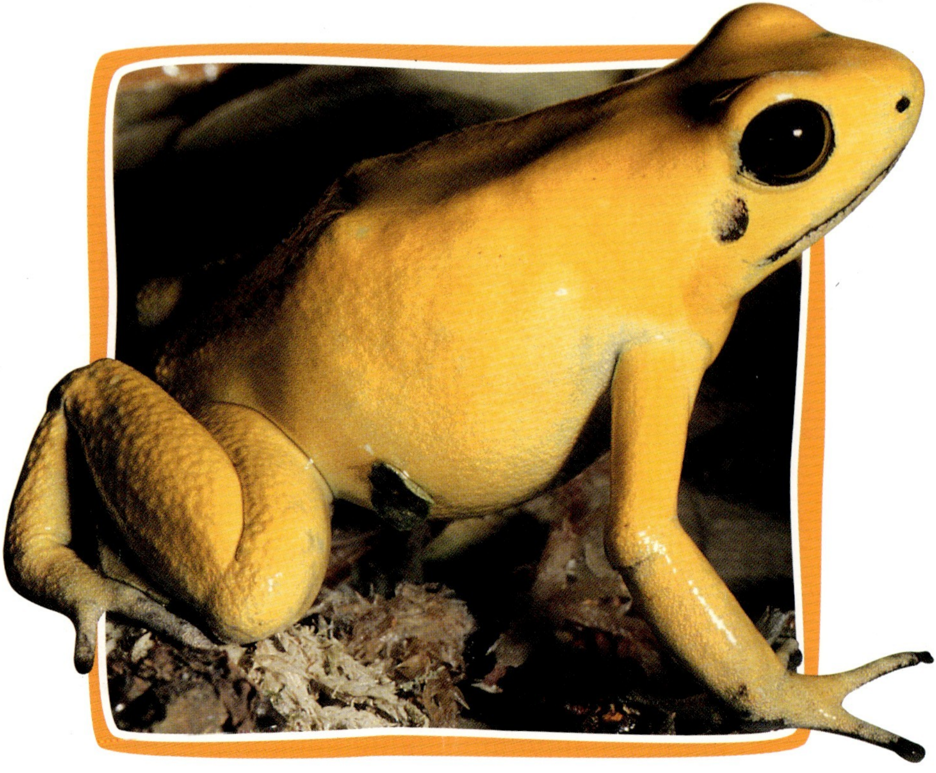

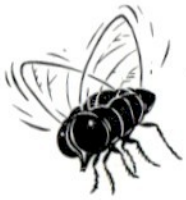

Ribbit!

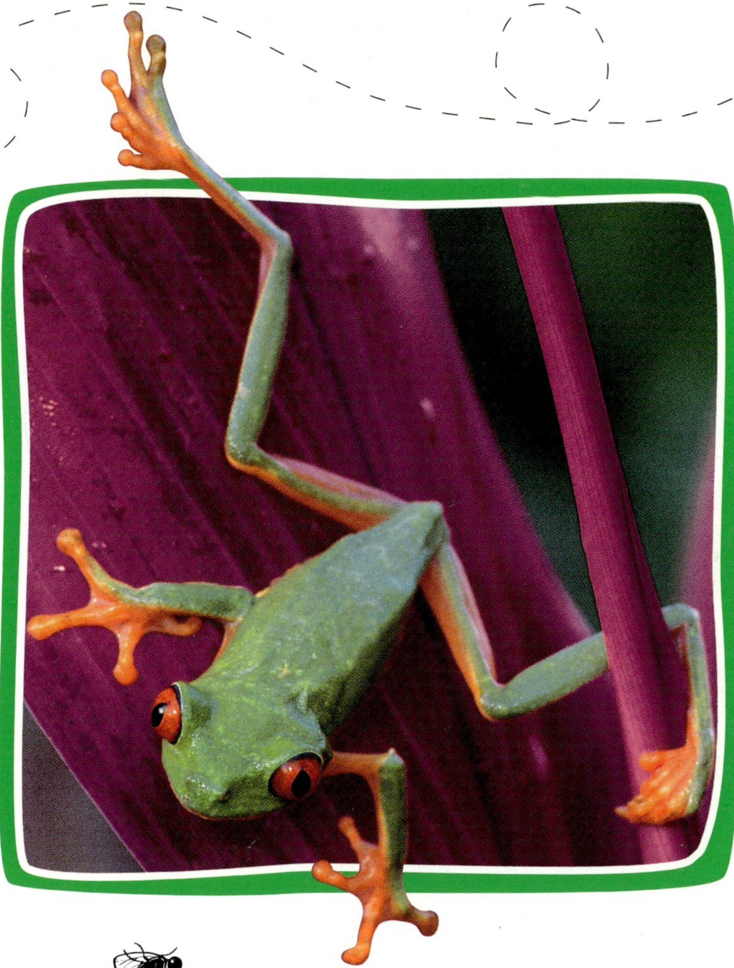

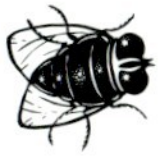

Ribbit!

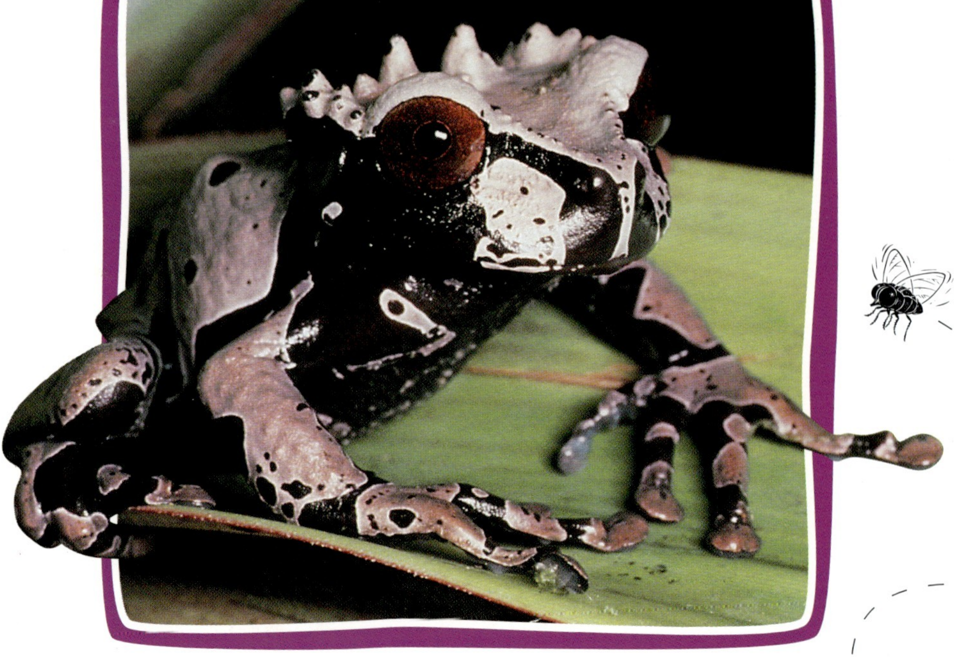

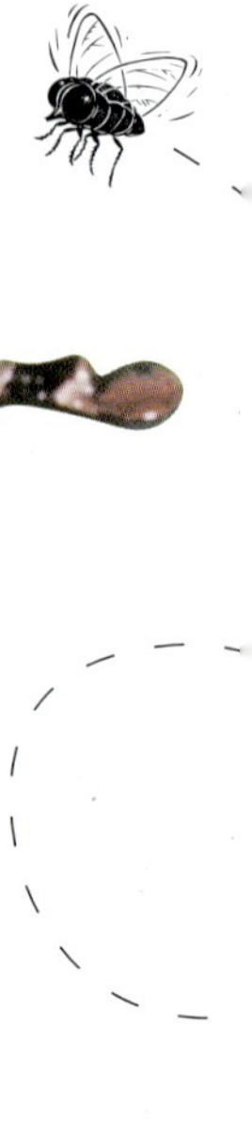

Ribbit!

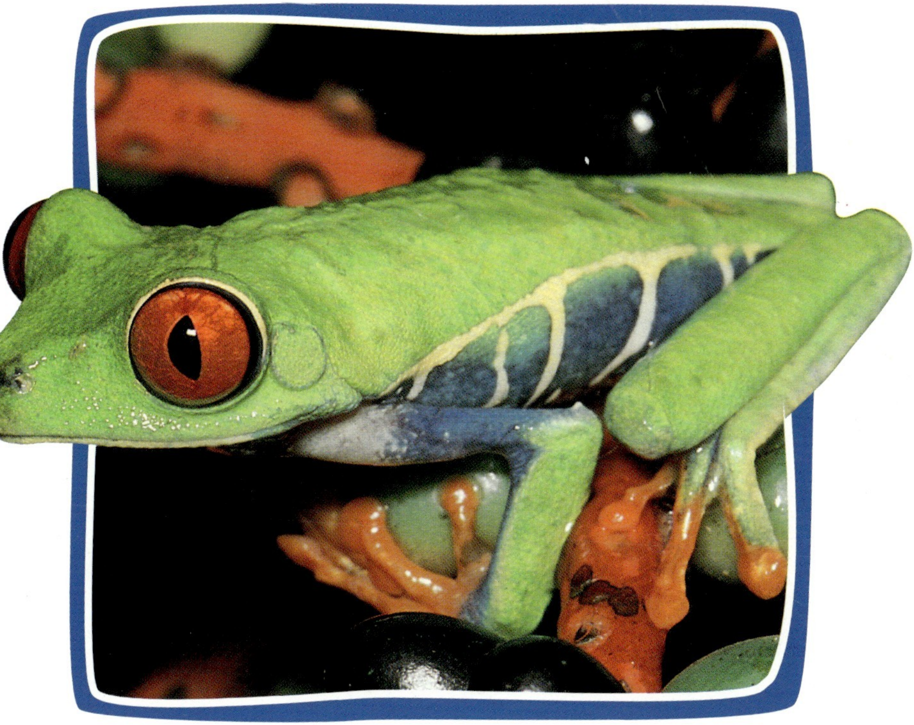

Ribbit!

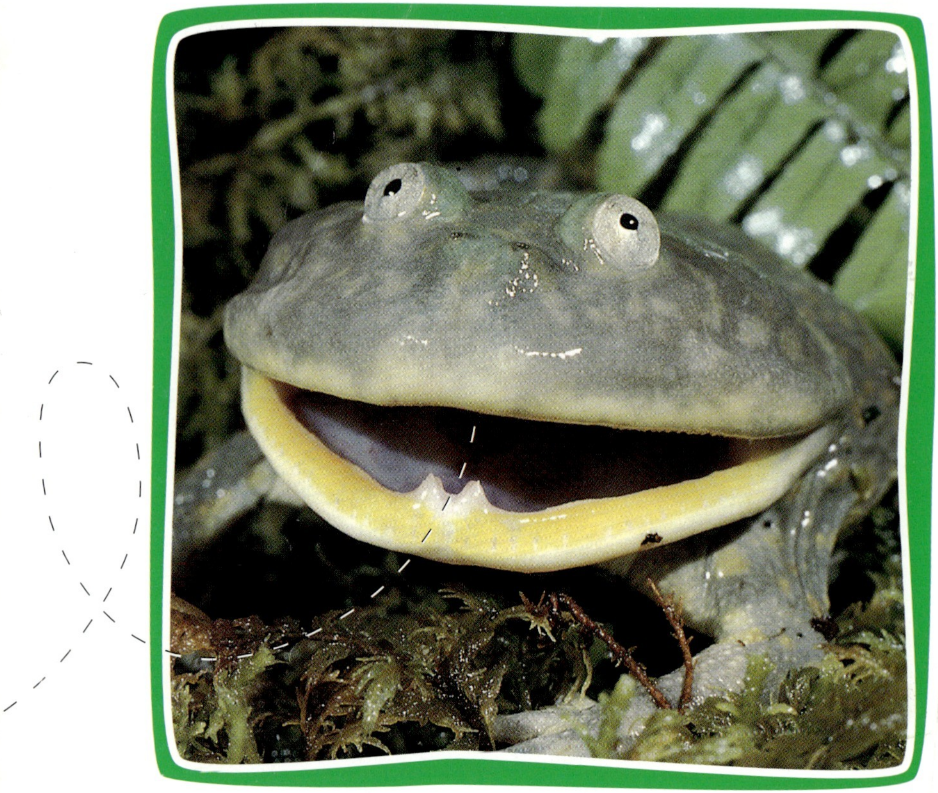

Gulp!